curiousabout

FLAG FOOTBALL

BY THOMAS K. AND HEATHER ADAMSON

AMICUS

What are you

curious about?

CHAPTER THREE

3

Playing the Game
PAGE
12

Curious About is published by Amicus
P.O. Box 227
Mankato, MN 56002
www.amicuspublishing.us

Editor: Alissa Thielges
Series Designer: Kathleen Petelinsek
Book Designer: Lori Bye
Photo Researchers: Omay Ayres

Library of Congress Cataloging-in-Publication Data
Names: Adamson, Thomas K., 1970- author.
| Adamson, Heather, 1974- author.
Title: Curious about football / by Thomas
K. and Heather Adamson.
Description: Mankato, MN: Amicus, [2024] | Series: Curious
about sports | Includes bibliographical references and index.
| Audience: Ages 6–9 | Audience: Grades 2–3 | Summary:
"Conversational questions and answers share what kids
can expect when they join a flag football team. A Stay
Curious! feature models research skills while simple
infographics support visual literacy"—Provided by publisher.
Identifiers: LCCN 2022039972 (print) | LCCN
2022039973 (ebook) | ISBN 9781645493228
(library binding) | ISBN 9781681528465
(paperback) | ISBN 9781645494102 (ebook)
Subjects: LCSH: Football—Juvenile literature.
Classification: LCC GV950.7.A329 2024 (print) | LCC
GV950.7 (ebook) | DDC 796.332—dc23/eng/20220916
LC record available at https://lccn.loc.gov/2022039972
LC ebook record available at https://lccn.loc.gov/2022039973

Photo credits: Alamy/ZUMA Press Inc 19; Dreamstime/
Derrick Neill 16, Sports Images 9, 15; Getty/Icon
Sportswire 20–21, The Washington Post 10; iStock/
gurineb cover, 1, 11, Joseph Calomeni 7; Shutterstock/
enterlinedesign 17 (background), JoeSAPhotos 4–5, 12–13

Printed in China

Do you need a helmet to play flag football?

No. Not all games need full gear. There is no tackling in flag football. All you need is a t-shirt, shorts, and **cleats**. In some **leagues**, you might need a mouth guard. Tackle football usually starts in middle school.

Many kids start with flag football to learn the basics of the sport.

DID YOU KNOW?
Flag football is growing more popular with girls. High schools and colleges have teams.

Why is the football shaped like that?

It's easier to carry and throw. An **oblong** ball flies nicely through the air. Flag football uses lots of passing plays. Teammates throw the ball to get closer to the **end zone**. That's where you score!

DID YOU KNOW?

To pass a football, grip the laces with your hand. The ball will spiral through the air. That helps it soar straight.

You need a strong arm to throw a football far.

CHAPTER TWO

How many players are on the field?

About five to nine players. It depends on the league and the age of the players. Each team has an **offense** and a **defense**. The offense has the ball and tries to score. The defense tries to stop the other team from scoring.

A runner darts around all the defense players.

Do you have to be big to play football?

Nope! Players of all sizes can join. They do not even need any football experience. Coaches teach the players skills and plays in practices. Flag football is a fast game. Run quick. Catch the ball. Or pull a flag!

Teams can have all boys, all girls, or a mix of both.

How do you "tackle" in flag football?

Grab the runner's flag! Two flags hang off each player's belt. The defense tries to pull a flag off whoever has the ball to stop them. No pushing or grabbing is allowed. The ball is placed where the flag was pulled.

DID YOU KNOW?

Runners can't hide or block their flag to keep from being tackled.

Speed is a player's
best chance against
defenders.

13

How do you score a touchdown?

By getting the ball into the end zone. To do this, the offense moves the ball down the field. The **quarterback** can hand the ball off or pass to a teammate. In flag football, the offense gets four plays to get to midfield. Then they get three plays to score a touchdown.

A quarterback throws the ball to her teammate.

CHIEFS

SCORING IN FLAG FOOTBALL

6
POINTS

Touchdown

2
POINTS

Safety

2
EXTRA
POINTS

Kick or pass
from 10 yards
(after touchdown)

1
EXTRA
POINT

Kick or pass
from 5 yards
(after touchdown)

A player hikes the ball to start a play.

What happens at the start of a play?

The **center** hikes the ball to the quarterback. The quarterback has seven seconds to pass or hand off the ball. On defense, **rushers** try to get to the quarterback. Each player has a job on each play.

FLAG FOOTBALL POSITIONS

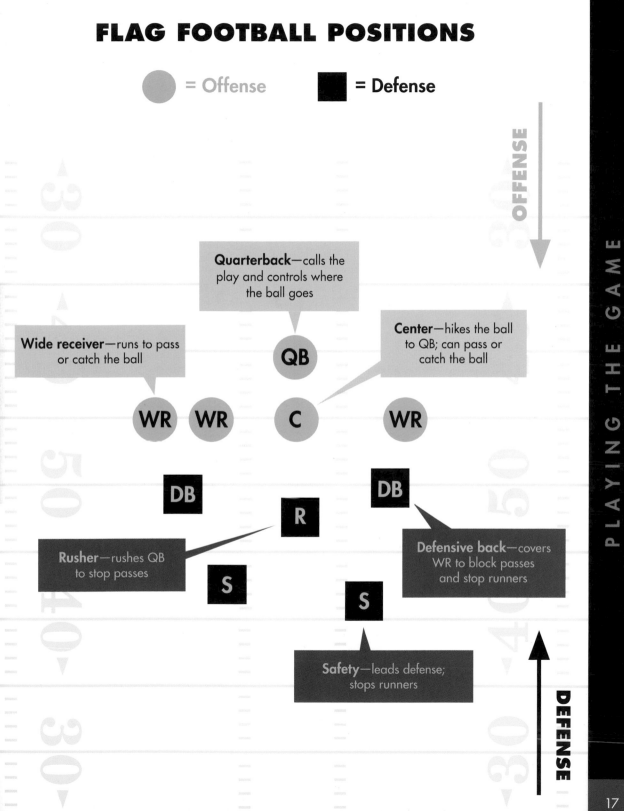

● = Offense   ■ = Defense

OFFENSE

Quarterback—calls the play and controls where the ball goes

Center—hikes the ball to QB; can pass or catch the ball

Wide receiver—runs to pass or catch the ball

QB

WR   WR   C   WR

DB   DB

R

Rusher—rushes QB to stop passes

S

Defensive back—covers WR to block passes and stop runners

S

Safety—leads defense; stops runners

DEFENSE

How else can the defense stop the offense?

The defense can **intercept** a pass. They also try to keep the runner from getting by them. Defenders move their feet quickly. They keep their heads up. They try to keep the offense from moving the ball down field.

DID YOU KNOW?
It's illegal to knock the ball out of a player's hands.

A boy jumps to intercept a throw.

Is football safe?

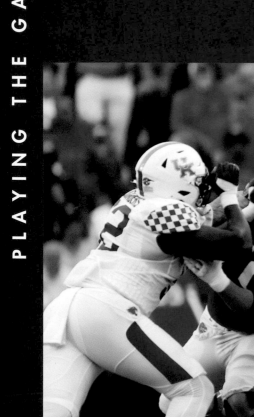

College players wear pads and helmets to stay safe.

There is no hitting or tackling in flag football. Players wear pads and gear for protection in tackle football. There are sometimes injuries. But people keep working on making it safer. Coaches teach the proper way to play the sport. Follow the rules to play the game well. That makes it the most fun!

ASK MORE QUESTIONS

What if a player drops a pass?

How do I find a team in my town?

Try a BIG QUESTION: How do football players stay safe while tackling?

SEARCH FOR ANSWERS

Search the library catalog or the Internet.
A librarian, teacher, or parent can help you.

Using Keywords
Find the looking glass.

🔍

Keywords are the most important words in your question.

?

If you want to know:

• what happens if a pass isn't caught, type: FLAG FOOTBALL FUMBLE RULES

• if your town has a team, type: FLAG FOOTBALL LEAGUES NEAR ME

FIND GOOD SOURCES

Here are some good, safe sources you can use in your research.
Your librarian can help you find more.

Books

Learning How to Play Flag Football
by Tammy Gagne, 2019.

On the Football Team
by Stephane Hillard, 2022.

Internet Sites

Discover Flag Football
https://playfootball.nfl.com/parents/discover-flag-football/
This site from the National Football League (NFL) has great information about why flag football is fun and safe.

NFL Flag Football
https://nflflag.com/
The NFL provides tons of information about flag football rules, plays, and practices.

Every effort has been made to ensure that these websites are appropriate for children. However, because of the nature of the Internet, it is impossible to guarantee that these sites will remain active indefinitely or that their contents will not be altered.

SHARE AND TAKE ACTION

Grab a football and play catch with a friend.

Watch other teams play games.
Watch the players at different positions to learn more about playing that position.

Search for videos online.
Find different ways to practice pulling a flag, or look for plays your team can learn.

GLOSSARY

center An offensive player, at the center of the line, who passes the ball to the quarterback at the start of each play.

cleats Shoes with knobs on the bottom that keep a player from sliding.

defense The group of players who try to stop the other team from scoring.

end zone The area at the ends of a football field where the ball goes to score points.

intercept To catch a pass made by the other team.

oblong Longer in one direction than the other.

offense The group of players who try to score points.

quarterback The player who leads the offense by directing the plays and controlling where the ball goes.

rusher A defensive player who runs around the offensive line to tackle the quarterback.

INDEX

About the Authors

Thomas K. and Heather Adamson are a husband-and-wife team who have written many books for kids. When they are not working, the couple likes to take hikes, watch movies, eat pizza, and of course, read. They live in South Dakota with their two sons and a Morkie dog named Moe.